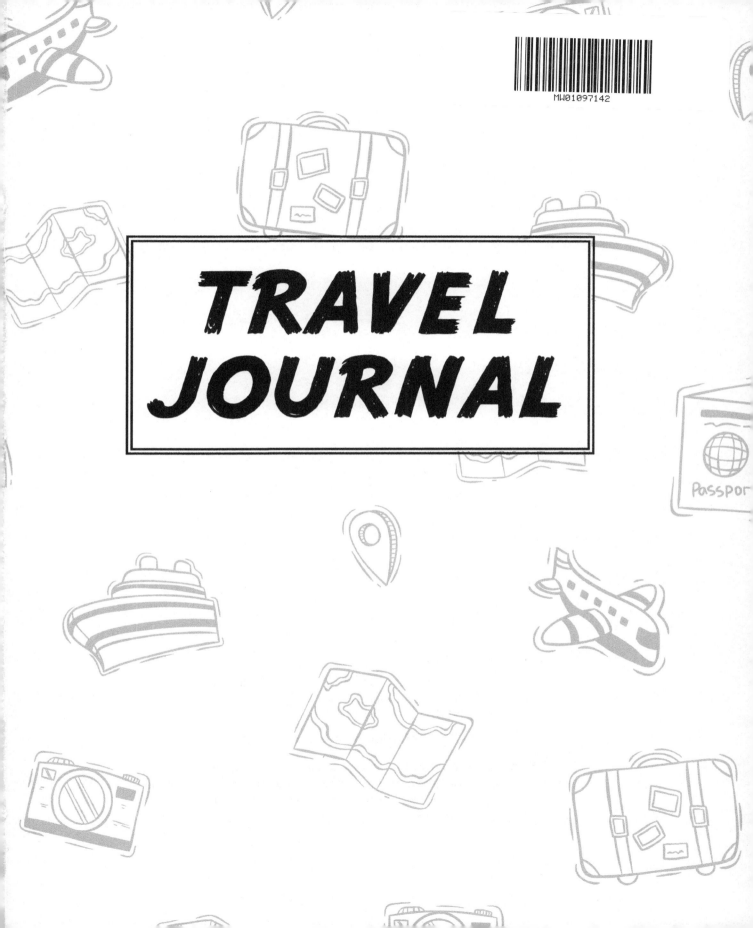

TRAVEL JOURNAL

First published in 2019 by Erin Rose Publishing

Text and illustration copyright © 2019 Erin Rose Publishing

Design: Julie Anson

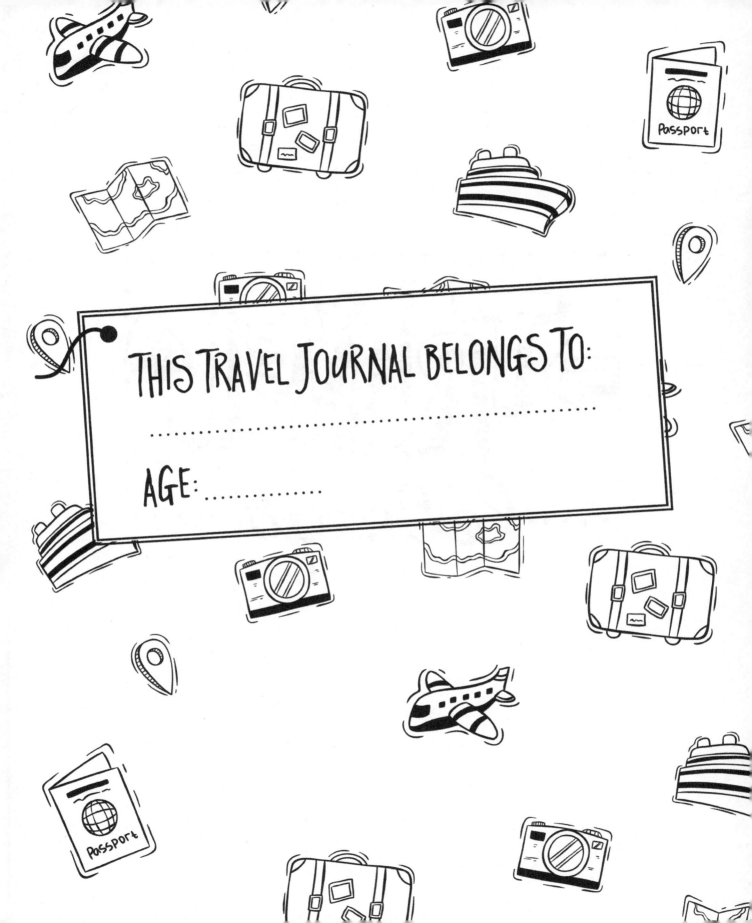

THIS TRAVEL JOURNAL BELONGS TO:

....

AGE: ....

My Adventure To: ....

MY JOURNEY STARTS AT: ....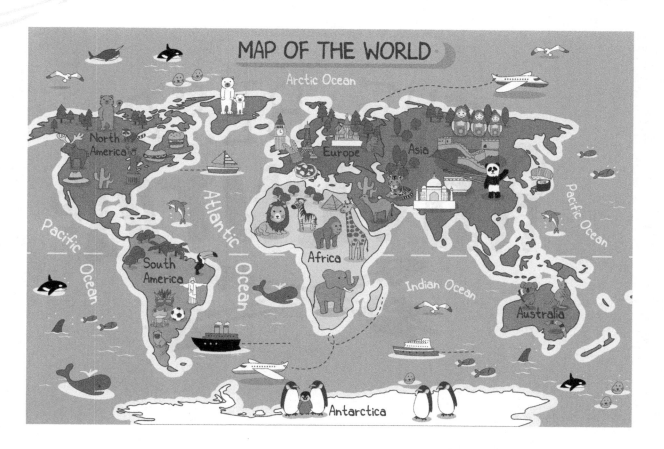

AND ENDS IN: ....

JANUARY	FEBRUARY	MARCH	APRIL	MAY	JUNE	JULY	AUGUST	SEPTEMBER	OCTOBER	NOVEMBER	DECEMBER

THE BEST
AdVENTUre

HOW LONG IS THE JOURNEY? ....

HOW AM I TRAVELLING? ....

WHERE AM I STAYING? ....

WHO IS GOING? ....

WHAT WOULD I LIKE TO DO WHEN I GET THERE? ....

....

....

....

....

....

WHAT AM I MOST LOOKING FORWARD TO? ....

....

....

....

WHAT DO I NEED TO PACK? YOU CAN WRITE YOUR PACKING LIST BELOW:

....

....

....

....

....

....

....

....

....

....

....

DATE:........................ LOCATION:................................... TODAY'S STAR RATING: ☆ ☆ ☆ ☆ ☆

TRAVELLED BY: ✈ PLANE ☐   🚢 BOAT ☐   🛣 ROAD ☐   🪧 WALK ☐   🎈 OTHER ☐

WHERE DID I VISIT?

WHO WAS THERE?

WHAT I DISCOVERED?

WHO DID I MEET?

MY FAVOURITE THING WAS:

MY MOOD WAS   😄 ☐   🙂 ☐   😐 ☐   🙁 ☐   😎 ☐   😴 ☐

WEATHER   ☀ ☐   ⛅ ☐   🌧 ☐   ⛈ ☐   🌧 ☐   🌨 ☐

PICTURE OF THE DAY

DRAW, SKETCH OR STICK-IN A PICTURE OR KEEPSAKE OF YOUR DAY.

DATE:........................ LOCATION:... TODAY'S STAR RATING: ☆ ☆ ☆ ☆ ☆

TRAVELLED BY: 🛩 PLANE ☐ 🚢 BOAT ☐ 🚗 ROAD ☐ 🪧 WALK ☐ 🎈 OTHER ☐

WHERE DID I VISIT?

WHO WAS THERE?

WHAT I DISCOVERED?

WHO DID I MEET?

MY FAVOURITE THING WAS:

MY MOOD WAS 😄 ☐ 🙂 ☐ 😐 ☐ 🙁 ☐ 😎 ☐ 😴 ☐

WEATHER ☀ ☐ ⛅ ☐ 🌥 ☐ ⛈ ☐ 🌧 ☐ 🌨 ☐

PICTURE OF THE DAY

DRAW, SKETCH OR STICK-IN A PICTURE OR KEEPSAKE OF YOUR DAY.

DATE:........................ LOCATION:... TODAY'S STAR RATING: ☆ ☆ ☆ ☆ ☆

TRAVELLED BY: ✈ [ ] 🚢 [ ] 🛣 [ ] 🪧 [ ] 🎈 [ ]
PLANE   BOAT   ROAD   WALK   OTHER

WHERE DID I VISIT?

WHO WAS THERE?

WHAT I DISCOVERED?

WHO DID I MEET?

MY FAVOURITE THING WAS:

MY MOOD WAS 😁 [ ] 🙂 [ ] 😐 [ ] 🙁 [ ] 😎 [ ] 😴 [ ]

WEATHER ☀ [ ] ⛅ [ ] 🌦 [ ] ⛈ [ ] 🌧 [ ] ❄ [ ]

PICTURE OF THE DAY

DRAW, SKETCH OR STICK-IN A PICTURE OR KEEPSAKE OF YOUR DAY.

DATE:........................ LOCATION:... TODAY'S STAR RATING: ☆ ☆ ☆ ☆ ☆

TRAVELLED BY: ✈ PLANE ☐   🚢 BOAT ☐   🛣 ROAD ☐   🪧 WALK ☐   🎈 OTHER ☐

WHERE DID I VISIT?

WHO WAS THERE?

WHAT I DISCOVERED?

WHO DID I MEET?

MY FAVOURITE THING WAS:

MY MOOD WAS 😄 ☐ 🙂 ☐ 😐 ☐ 🙁 ☐ 😎 ☐ 😴 ☐

WEATHER ☀ ☐ ⛅ ☐ 🌥 ☐ ⛈ ☐ 🌧 ☐ 🌨 ☐

PICTURE OF THE DAY

DRAW, SKETCH OR STICK-IN A PICTURE OR KEEPSAKE OF YOUR DAY.

DATE:........................ LOCATION:.. TODAY'S STAR RATING: ☆☆☆☆☆

TRAVELLED BY: ✈ PLANE ☐ 🚢 BOAT ☐ 🛣 ROAD ☐ 🪧 WALK ☐ 🎈 OTHER ☐

WHERE DID I VISIT?

WHO WAS THERE?

WHAT I DISCOVERED?

WHO DID I MEET?

MY FAVOURITE THING WAS:

MY MOOD WAS 😄 ☐ 🙂 ☐ 😐 ☐ 🙁 ☐ 😎 ☐ 😴 ☐

WEATHER ☀ ☐ ⛅ ☐ 🌦 ☐ ⛈ ☐ 🌧 ☐ 🌨 ☐

PICTURE OF THE DAY

DRAW, SKETCH OR STICK-IN A PICTURE OR KEEPSAKE OF YOUR DAY.

DATE: .... LOCATION: .... TODAY'S STAR RATING: ☆☆☆☆☆

TRAVELLED BY: ✈ PLANE ☐ 🚢 BOAT ☐ 🛣 ROAD ☐ 🪧 WALK ☐ 🎈 OTHER ☐

WHERE DID I VISIT?

WHO WAS THERE?

WHAT I DISCOVERED?

WHO DID I MEET?

MY FAVOURITE THING WAS:

MY MOOD WAS 😄 ☐ 🙂 ☐ 😐 ☐ 🙁 ☐ 😎 ☐ 😴 ☐

WEATHER ☀ ☐ ⛅ ☐ 🌥 ☐ ⛈ ☐ 🌧 ☐ 🌨 ☐

PICTURE OF THE DAY

DRAW, SKETCH OR STICK-IN A PICTURE OR KEEPSAKE OF YOUR DAY.

DATE:........................ LOCATION:.. TODAY'S STAR RATING: ☆☆☆☆☆

TRAVELLED BY: ✈ ☐ 🚢 ☐ 🛤 ☐ 🪧 ☐ 🎈 ☐
PLANE   BOAT   ROAD   WALK   OTHER

WHERE DID I VISIT?

WHO WAS THERE?

WHAT I DISCOVERED?

_ DID I MEET?

_RITE THING WAS:

😛 ☐ 🙂 ☐ 😐 ☐ 🙁 ☐ 😎 ☐ 😴 ☐

☐ 🌤 ☐ 🌦 ☐ ⛈ ☐ 🌧 ☐ 🌨 ☐

PICTURE OF THE DAY

DRAW, SKETCH OR STICK-IN A PICTURE OR KEEPSAKE OF YOUR DAY.

DATE:........................ LOCATION:.. TODAY'S STAR RATING: ☆☆☆☆☆

TRAVELLED BY: ✈ □ 🚢 □ 🛣 □ 🪧 □ 🎈 □
PLANE   BOAT   ROAD   WALK   OTHER

WHERE DID I VISIT?

WHO WAS THERE?

WHAT I DISCOVERED?

WHO DID I MEET?

MY FAVOURITE THING WAS:

MY MOOD WAS 😄 □ 🙂 □ 😐 □ 🙁 □ 😎 □ 😴 □

WEATHER ☀ □ ⛅ □ 🌦 □ ⛈ □ 🌧 □ 🌨 □

PICTURE OF THE DAY

DRAW, SKETCH OR STICK-IN A PICTURE OR KEEPSAKE OF YOUR DAY.

DATE:........................ LOCATION:.. TODAY'S STAR RATING: ☆ ☆ ☆ ☆ ☆

TRAVELLED BY: ✈ PLANE ☐ 🚢 BOAT ☐ 🛣 ROAD ☐ 🪧 WALK ☐ 🎈 OTHER ☐

WHERE DID I VISIT?

WHO WAS THERE?

WHAT I DISCOVERED?

WHO DID I MEET?

MY FAVOURITE THING WAS:

MY MOOD WAS 😄 ☐ 🙂 ☐ 😐 ☐ ☹ ☐ 😎 ☐ 😴 ☐

WEATHER ☀ ☐ ⛅ ☐ 🌦 ☐ ⛈ ☐ 🌧 ☐ ❄ ☐

PICTURE OF THE DAY

DRAW, SKETCH OR STICK-IN A PICTURE OR KEEPSAKE OF YOUR DAY.

DATE:........................ LOCATION:.. TODAY'S STAR RATING: ☆ ☆ ☆ ☆ ☆

TRAVELLED BY: ✈ ☐ 🚢 ☐ 🛣 ☐ 🪧 ☐ 🎈 ☐
PLANE   BOAT   ROAD   WALK   OTHER

WHERE DID I VISIT?

WHO WAS THERE?

WHAT I DISCOVERED?

WHO DID I MEET?

MY FAVOURITE THING WAS:

MY MOOD WAS 😄 ☐ 🙂 ☐ 😐 ☐ 🙁 ☐ 😎 ☐ 😴 ☐

WEATHER ☀ ☐ ⛅ ☐ 🌥 ☐ ⛈ ☐ 🌧 ☐ 🌨 ☐

PICTURE OF THE DAY

DRAW, SKETCH OR STICK-IN A PICTURE OR KEEPSAKE OF YOUR DAY.

DATE:........................ LOCATION:... TODAY'S STAR RATING: ☆ ☆ ☆ ☆ ☆

TRAVELLED BY: ✈ ☐ 🚢 ☐ 🔥 ☐ 🪧 ☐ 🎈 ☐
PLANE   BOAT   ROAD   WALK   OTHER

WHERE DID I VISIT?

WHO WAS THERE?

WHAT I DISCOVERED?

WHO DID I MEET?

MY FAVOURITE THING WAS:

MY MOOD WAS 😄 ☐ 🙂 ☐ 😐 ☐ ☹ ☐ 😎 ☐ 😴 ☐

WEATHER ☀ ☐ ⛅ ☐ 🌦 ☐ ⛈ ☐ 🌧 ☐ ❄ ☐

PICTURE OF THE DAY

DRAW, SKETCH OR STICK-IN A PICTURE OR KEEPSAKE OF YOUR DAY.

DATE:................... LOCATION:................................. TODAY'S STAR RATING: ☆☆☆☆☆

TRAVELLED BY: ✈ ☐ 🚢 ☐ 🛣 ☐ 🪧 ☐ 🎈 ☐
PLANE   BOAT   ROAD   WALK   OTHER

WHERE DID I VISIT?

WHO WAS THERE?

WHAT I DISCOVERED?

WHO DID I MEET?

MY FAVOURITE THING WAS:

MY MOOD WAS 😄☐ 🙂☐ 😐☐ ☹️☐ 😎☐ 😴☐

WEATHER ☀️☐ ⛅☐ 🌦☐ ⛈☐ 🌧☐ 🌨☐

PICTURE OF THE DAY

DRAW, SKETCH OR STICK-IN A PICTURE OR KEEPSAKE OF YOUR DAY.

DATE:..................... LOCATION:... TODAY'S STAR RATING: ☆ ☆ ☆ ☆ ☆

TRAVELLED BY: PLANE ☐ BOAT ☐ ROAD ☐ WALK ☐ OTHER ☐

WHERE DID I VISIT?

WHO WAS THERE?

WHAT I DISCOVERED?

WHO DID I MEET?

MY FAVOURITE THING WAS:

MY MOOD WAS 😄 ☐ 🙂 ☐ 😐 ☐ ☹️ ☐ 😎 ☐ 😴 ☐

WEATHER ☀️ ☐ ⛅ ☐ 🌥️ ☐ ⛈️ ☐ 🌧️ ☐ ❄️ ☐

PICTURE OF THE DAY

DRAW, SKETCH OR STICK-IN A PICTURE OR KEEPSAKE OF YOUR DAY.

DATE:...................... LOCATION:.................................... TODAY'S STAR RATING: ☆ ☆ ☆ ☆ ☆

TRAVELLED BY: 🛩 ☐   🚢 ☐   🛣 ☐   🪧 ☐   🎈 ☐

               PLANE   BOAT   ROAD   WALK   OTHER

WHERE DID I VISIT?

WHO WAS THERE?

WHAT I DISCOVERED?

WHO DID I MEET?

MY FAVOURITE THING WAS:

MY MOOD WAS   😄 ☐   🙂 ☐   😐 ☐   ☹ ☐   😎 ☐   😴 ☐

WEATHER   ☀ ☐   ⛅ ☐   🌥 ☐   ⛈ ☐   🌧 ☐   🌨 ☐

PICTURE OF THE DAY

DRAW, SKETCH OR STICK-IN A PICTURE OR KEEPSAKE OF YOUR DAY.

DATE:........................ LOCATION:.. TODAY'S STAR RATING: ☆☆☆☆☆

TRAVELLED BY: ✈ ☐ PLANE 🚢 ☐ BOAT 🛣 ☐ ROAD 🪧 ☐ WALK 🎈 ☐ OTHER

WHERE DID I VISIT?

WHO WAS THERE?

WHAT I DISCOVERED?

WHO DID I MEET?

MY FAVOURITE THING WAS:

MY MOOD WAS 😄 ☐ 🙂 ☐ 😐 ☐ ☹ ☐ 😎 ☐ 😴 ☐

WEATHER ☀ ☐ ⛅ ☐ 🌦 ☐ ⛈ ☐ 🌧 ☐ 🌨 ☐

PICTURE OF THE DAY

DRAW, SKETCH OR STICK-IN A PICTURE OR KEEPSAKE OF YOUR DAY.

DATE:...................... LOCATION:.. TODAY'S STAR RATING: ☆ ☆ ☆ ☆ ☆

TRAVELLED BY: ✈ ☐ 🚢 ☐ 🛣 ☐ 🪧 ☐ 🎈 ☐
PLANE BOAT ROAD WALK OTHER

WHERE DID I VISIT?

WHO WAS THERE?

WHAT I DISCOVERED?

WHO DID I MEET?

MY FAVOURITE THING WAS:

MY MOOD WAS 😄 ☐ 🙂 ☐ 😐 ☐ 🙁 ☐ 😎 ☐ 😴 ☐

WEATHER ☀ ☐ ⛅ ☐ 🌥 ☐ ⛈ ☐ 🌧 ☐ 🌨 ☐

PICTURE OF THE DAY

DRAW, SKETCH OR STICK-IN A PICTURE OR KEEPSAKE OF YOUR DAY.

DATE:.................... LOCATION:.. TODAY'S STAR RATING: ☆ ☆ ☆ ☆ ☆

TRAVELLED BY: ✈ ☐   🚢 ☐   🔥 ☐   🪧 ☐   🎈 ☐
PLANE   BOAT   ROAD   WALK   OTHER

WHERE DID I VISIT?

WHO WAS THERE?

WHAT I DISCOVERED?

WHO DID I MEET?

MY FAVOURITE THING WAS:

MY MOOD WAS 😄 ☐ 🙂 ☐ 😐 ☐ 🙁 ☐ 😎 ☐ 😴 ☐

WEATHER ☀ ☐ ⛅ ☐ 🌥 ☐ ⛈ ☐ 🌧 ☐ 🌨 ☐

PICTURE OF THE DAY

DRAW, SKETCH OR STICK-IN A PICTURE OR KEEPSAKE OF YOUR DAY.

DATE:........................ LOCATION:.. TODAY'S STAR RATING: ☆ ☆ ☆ ☆ ☆

TRAVELLED BY: ✈ □   🚢 □   🛣 □   🪧 □   🎈 □
           PLANE   BOAT   ROAD   WALK   OTHER

WHERE DID I VISIT?

WHO WAS THERE?

WHAT I DISCOVERED?

WHO DID I MEET?

MY FAVOURITE THING WAS:

MY MOOD WAS   😄 □   🙂 □   😐 □   ☹ □   😎 □   😴 □

WEATHER   ☀ □   ⛅ □   🌥 □   ⛈ □   🌧 □   🌨 □

PICTURE OF THE DAY

DRAW, SKETCH OR STICK-IN A PICTURE OR KEEPSAKE OF YOUR DAY.

DATE:.................... LOCATION:... TODAY'S STAR RATING: ☆ ☆ ☆ ☆ ☆

TRAVELLED BY: ✈ ☐ 🚢 ☐ 🔥 ☐ 🪧 ☐ 🎈 ☐
PLANE   BOAT   ROAD   WALK   OTHER

WHERE DID I VISIT?

WHO WAS THERE?

WHAT I DISCOVERED?

WHO DID I MEET?

MY FAVOURITE THING WAS:

MY MOOD WAS 😄 ☐ 🙂 ☐ 😐 ☐ 🙁 ☐ 😎 ☐ 😴 ☐

WEATHER ☀ ☐ ⛅ ☐ 🌥 ☐ ⛈ ☐ 🌧 ☐ ❄ ☐

PICTURE OF THE DAY

DRAW, SKETCH OR STICK-IN A PICTURE OR KEEPSAKE OF YOUR DAY.

DATE:........................ LOCATION:... TODAY'S STAR RATING: ☆☆☆☆☆

TRAVELLED BY: ✈ ☐ 🚢 ☐ 🛣 ☐ 🪧 ☐ 🎈 ☐
PLANE   BOAT   ROAD   WALK   OTHER

WHERE DID I VISIT?

WHO WAS THERE?

WHAT I DISCOVERED?

WHO DID I MEET?

MY FAVOURITE THING WAS:

MY MOOD WAS 😄 ☐ 🙂 ☐ 😐 ☐ 🙁 ☐ 😎 ☐ 😴 ☐

WEATHER ☀ ☐ ⛅ ☐ 🌦 ☐ ⛈ ☐ 🌧 ☐ 🌨 ☐

PICTURE OF THE DAY

DRAW, SKETCH OR STICK-IN A PICTURE OR KEEPSAKE OF YOUR DAY.

DATE:................. LOCATION:................................ TODAY'S STAR RATING: ☆ ☆ ☆ ☆ ☆

TRAVELLED BY: PLANE ☐ BOAT ☐ ROAD ☐ WALK ☐ OTHER ☐

WHERE DID I VISIT?

WHO WAS THERE?

WHAT I DISCOVERED?

WHO DID I MEET?

MY FAVOURITE THING WAS:

MY MOOD WAS 😄 ☐ 🙂 ☐ 😐 ☐ 🙁 ☐ 😎 ☐ 😴 ☐

WEATHER ☀ ☐ ⛅ ☐ 🌦 ☐ ⛈ ☐ 🌧 ☐ 🌨 ☐

PICTURE OF THE DAY

DRAW, SKETCH OR STICK-IN A PICTURE OR KEEPSAKE OF YOUR DAY.

DATE:................................ LOCATION:.. TODAY'S STAR RATING: ☆☆☆☆☆

TRAVELLED BY: ✈ PLANE ☐ 🚢 BOAT ☐ 🛣 ROAD ☐ 🪧 WALK ☐ 🎈 OTHER ☐

WHERE DID I VISIT?

WHO WAS THERE?

WHAT I DISCOVERED?

WHO DID I MEET?

MY FAVOURITE THING WAS:

MY MOOD WAS 😄 ☐ 🙂 ☐ 😐 ☐ 🙁 ☐ 😎 ☐ 😴 ☐

WEATHER ☀ ☐ ⛅ ☐ 🌥 ☐ ⛈ ☐ 🌧 ☐ 🌨 ☐

PICTURE OF THE DAY

DRAW, SKETCH OR STICK-IN A PICTURE OR KEEPSAKE OF YOUR DAY.

DATE:.................... LOCATION:................................. TODAY'S STAR RATING: ☆☆☆☆☆

TRAVELLED BY: ✈ ☐ 🚢 ☐ 🔥 ☐ 🪧 ☐ 🎈 ☐
PLANE   BOAT   ROAD   WALK   OTHER

WHERE DID I VISIT?

WHO WAS THERE?

WHAT I DISCOVERED?

WHO DID I MEET?

MY FAVOURITE THING WAS:

MY MOOD WAS 😄 ☐ 🙂 ☐ 😐 ☐ 🙁 ☐ 😎 ☐ 😴 ☐

WEATHER ☀ ☐ ⛅ ☐ 🌦 ☐ ⛈ ☐ 🌧 ☐ 🌨 ☐

PICTURE OF THE DAY

DRAW, SKETCH OR STICK-IN A PICTURE OR KEEPSAKE OF YOUR DAY.

DATE:........................ LOCATION:.................................... TODAY'S STAR RATING: ☆☆☆☆☆

TRAVELLED BY: ✈ PLANE ☐ 🚢 BOAT ☐ 🛣 ROAD ☐ 🪧 WALK ☐ 🎈 OTHER ☐

WHERE DID I VISIT?

WHO WAS THERE?

WHAT I DISCOVERED?

WHO DID I MEET?

MY FAVOURITE THING WAS:

MY MOOD WAS 😄 ☐ 🙂 ☐ 😐 ☐ 🙁 ☐ 😎 ☐ 😴 ☐

WEATHER ☀ ☐ ⛅ ☐ 🌦 ☐ ⛈ ☐ 🌧 ☐ 🌨 ☐

PICTURE OF THE DAY

DRAW, SKETCH OR STICK-IN A PICTURE OR KEEPSAKE OF YOUR DAY.

DATE:........................ LOCATION:.. TODAY'S STAR RATING: ☆ ☆ ☆ ☆ ☆

TRAVELLED BY: PLANE ☐ BOAT ☐ ROAD ☐ WALK ☐ OTHER ☐

WHERE DID I VISIT?

WHO WAS THERE?

WHAT I DISCOVERED?

WHO DID I MEET?

MY FAVOURITE THING WAS:

MY MOOD WAS 😄 ☐ 🙂 ☐ 😐 ☐ 🙁 ☐ 😎 ☐ 😴 ☐

WEATHER ☀ ☐ ⛅ ☐ 🌥 ☐ ⛈ ☐ 🌧 ☐ ❄ ☐

PICTURE OF THE DAY

DRAW, SKETCH OR STICK-IN A PICTURE OR KEEPSAKE OF YOUR DAY.

DATE: .... LOCATION: .... TODAY'S STAR RATING: ☆ ☆ ☆ ☆ ☆

TRAVELLED BY: ✈ ☐ 🚢 ☐ 🛣 ☐ 🪧 ☐ 🎈 ☐
PLANE   BOAT   ROAD   WALK   OTHER

WHERE DID I VISIT?

WHO WAS THERE?

WHAT I DISCOVERED?

WHO DID I MEET?

MY FAVOURITE THING WAS:

MY MOOD WAS   😄 ☐ 🙂 ☐ 😐 ☐ ☹ ☐ 😎 ☐ 😴 ☐

WEATHER   ☀ ☐ ⛅ ☐ 🌤 ☐ ⛈ ☐ 🌧 ☐ 🌨 ☐

PICTURE OF THE DAY

DRAW, SKETCH OR STICK-IN A PICTURE OR KEEPSAKE OF YOUR DAY.

DATE:................... LOCATION:.. TODAY'S STAR RATING: ☆☆☆☆☆

TRAVELLED BY: ✈ PLANE ☐ 🚢 BOAT ☐ 🛣 ROAD ☐ 🪧 WALK ☐ 🎈 OTHER ☐

WHERE DID I VISIT?

WHO WAS THERE?

WHAT I DISCOVERED?

WHO DID I MEET?

MY FAVOURITE THING WAS:

MY MOOD WAS 😄 ☐ 🙂 ☐ 😐 ☐ 🙁 ☐ 😎 ☐ 😴 ☐

WEATHER ☀ ☐ ⛅ ☐ 🌦 ☐ ⛈ ☐ 🌧 ☐ 🌨 ☐

PICTURE OF THE DAY

DRAW, SKETCH OR STICK-IN A PICTURE OR KEEPSAKE OF YOUR DAY.

DATE: .... LOCATION: .... TODAY'S STAR RATING: ☆☆☆☆☆

TRAVELLED BY: ✈ PLANE ☐ 🚢 BOAT ☐ 🛣 ROAD ☐ 🪧 WALK ☐ 🎈 OTHER ☐

WHERE DID I VISIT?

WHO WAS THERE?

WHAT I DISCOVERED?

WHO DID I MEET?

MY FAVOURITE THING WAS:

MY MOOD WAS 😄 ☐ 🙂 ☐ 😐 ☐ 🙁 ☐ 😎 ☐ 😴 ☐

WEATHER ☀ ☐ ⛅ ☐ 🌥 ☐ ⛈ ☐ 🌧 ☐ 🌨 ☐

PICTURE OF THE DAY

DRAW, SKETCH OR STICK-IN A PICTURE OR KEEPSAKE OF YOUR DAY.

DATE:........................ LOCATION:.. TODAY'S STAR RATING: ☆☆☆☆☆

TRAVELLED BY: ✈ PLANE ☐ 🚢 BOAT ☐ 🛣 ROAD ☐ 🪧 WALK ☐ 🎈 OTHER ☐

WHERE DID I VISIT?

WHO WAS THERE?

WHAT I DISCOVERED?

WHO DID I MEET?

MY FAVOURITE THING WAS:

MY MOOD WAS 😄 ☐ 🙂 ☐ 😐 ☐ ☹ ☐ 😎 ☐ 😴 ☐

WEATHER ☀ ☐ ⛅ ☐ 🌦 ☐ ⛈ ☐ 🌧 ☐ 🌨 ☐

PICTURE OF THE DAY

DRAW, SKETCH OR STICK-IN A PICTURE OR KEEPSAKE OF YOUR DAY.

DATE: .... LOCATION: .... TODAY'S STAR RATING: ☆ ☆ ☆ ☆ ☆

TRAVELLED BY: ✈ □ PLANE   🚢 □ BOAT   🛣 □ ROAD   🪧 □ WALK   🎈 □ OTHER

WHERE DID I VISIT?

WHO WAS THERE?

WHAT I DISCOVERED?

WHO DID I MEET?

MY FAVOURITE THING WAS:

MY MOOD WAS   😄 □   🙂 □   😐 □   🙁 □   😎 □   😴 □

WEATHER   ☀ □   ⛅ □   🌦 □   ⛈ □   🌧 □   🌨 □

PICTURE OF THE DAY

DRAW, SKETCH OR STICK-IN A PICTURE OR KEEPSAKE OF YOUR DAY.

DATE:............................ LOCATION:... TODAY'S STAR RATING: ☆☆☆☆☆

TRAVELLED BY: ✈ ☐ 🚢 ☐ 🛣 ☐ 🪧 ☐ 🎈 ☐
PLANE   BOAT   ROAD   WALK   OTHER

WHERE DID I VISIT?

WHO WAS THERE?

WHAT I DISCOVERED?

WHO DID I MEET?

MY FAVOURITE THING WAS:

MY MOOD WAS 😄 ☐ 🙂 ☐ 😐 ☐ 🙁 ☐ 😎 ☐ 😴 ☐

WEATHER ☀ ☐ ⛅ ☐ 🌦 ☐ ⛈ ☐ 🌧 ☐ ❄ ☐

PICTURE OF THE DAY

DRAW, SKETCH OR STICK-IN A PICTURE OR KEEPSAKE OF YOUR DAY.

DATE: .... LOCATION: .... TODAY'S STAR RATING: ☆☆☆☆☆

TRAVELLED BY: ✈ PLANE ☐ 🚢 BOAT ☐ 🛣 ROAD ☐ 🪧 WALK ☐ 🎈 OTHER ☐

WHERE DID I VISIT?

WHO WAS THERE?

WHAT I DISCOVERED?

WHO DID I MEET?

MY FAVOURITE THING WAS:

MY MOOD WAS 😄 ☐ 🙂 ☐ 😐 ☐ 🙁 ☐ 😎 ☐ 😴 ☐

WEATHER ☀ ☐ ⛅ ☐ 🌧 ☐ ⛈ ☐ 🌧 ☐ 🌨 ☐

PICTURE OF THE DAY

DRAW, SKETCH OR STICK-IN A PICTURE OR KEEPSAKE OF YOUR DAY.

DATE:............................ LOCATION:.. TODAY'S STAR RATING: ☆ ☆ ☆ ☆ ☆

TRAVELLED BY: PLANE ☐   BOAT ☐   ROAD ☐   WALK ☐   OTHER ☐

WHERE DID I VISIT?

WHO WAS THERE?

WHAT I DISCOVERED?

WHO DID I MEET?

MY FAVOURITE THING WAS:

MY MOOD WAS 😄 ☐ 🙂 ☐ 😐 ☐ ☹️ ☐ 😎 ☐ 😴 ☐

WEATHER ☀️ ☐ ⛅ ☐ 🌥️ ☐ ⛈️ ☐ 🌧️ ☐ ❄️ ☐

PICTURE OF THE DAY

DRAW, SKETCH OR STICK-IN A PICTURE OR KEEPSAKE OF YOUR DAY.

DATE: ....   LOCATION: ....   TODAY'S STAR RATING: ☆ ☆ ☆ ☆ ☆

TRAVELLED BY: ✈ ☐   🚢 ☐   🛣 ☐   🪧 ☐   🎈 ☐
     PLANE   BOAT   ROAD   WALK   OTHER

WHERE DID I VISIT?

WHO WAS THERE?

WHAT I DISCOVERED?

WHO DID I MEET?

MY FAVOURITE THING WAS:

MY MOOD WAS   😄 ☐   🙂 ☐   😐 ☐   🙁 ☐   😎 ☐   😴 ☐

WEATHER   ☀ ☐   ⛅ ☐   🌥 ☐   ⛈ ☐   🌧 ☐   🌨 ☐

PICTURE OF THE DAY

DRAW, SKETCH OR STICK-IN A PICTURE OR KEEPSAKE OF YOUR DAY.

DATE: .... LOCATION: .... TODAY'S STAR RATING: ☆ ☆ ☆ ☆ ☆

TRAVELLED BY: ✈ PLANE ☐ 🚢 BOAT ☐ 🛣 ROAD ☐ 🪧 WALK ☐ 🎈 OTHER ☐

WHERE DID I VISIT?

WHO WAS THERE?

WHAT I DISCOVERED?

WHO DID I MEET?

MY FAVOURITE THING WAS:

MY MOOD WAS 😄 ☐ 🙂 ☐ 😐 ☐ 🙁 ☐ 😎 ☐ 😴 ☐

WEATHER ☀ ☐ ⛅ ☐ 🌥 ☐ ⛈ ☐ 🌧 ☐ 🌨 ☐

PICTURE OF THE DAY

DRAW, SKETCH OR STICK-IN A PICTURE OR KEEPSAKE OF YOUR DAY.

DATE: .... LOCATION: .... TODAY'S STAR RATING: ☆☆☆☆☆

TRAVELLED BY: ✈ □ 🚢 □ 🛣 □ 🪧 □ 🎈 □
PLANE   BOAT   ROAD   WALK   OTHER

WHERE DID I VISIT?

WHO WAS THERE?

WHAT I DISCOVERED?

WHO DID I MEET?

MY FAVOURITE THING WAS:

MY MOOD WAS 😄 □ 🙂 □ 😐 □ ☹ □ 😎 □ 😴 □

WEATHER ☀ □ ⛅ □ 🌥 □ ⛈ □ 🌧 □ 🌨 □

PICTURE OF THE DAY

DRAW, SKETCH OR STICK-IN A PICTURE OR KEEPSAKE OF YOUR DAY.

DATE:............................ LOCATION:.. TODAY'S STAR RATING: ☆ ☆ ☆ ☆ ☆

TRAVELLED BY: ✈ PLANE ☐ 🛳 BOAT ☐ 🚗 ROAD ☐ 🪧 WALK ☐ 🎈 OTHER ☐

WHERE DID I VISIT?

WHO WAS THERE?

WHAT I DISCOVERED?

WHO DID I MEET?

MY FAVOURITE THING WAS:

MY MOOD WAS 😄 ☐ 🙂 ☐ 😐 ☐ 🙁 ☐ 😎 ☐ 😴 ☐

WEATHER ☀ ☐ ⛅ ☐ 🌦 ☐ ⛈ ☐ 🌧 ☐ 🌨 ☐

PICTURE OF THE DAY

DRAW, SKETCH OR STICK-IN A PICTURE OR KEEPSAKE OF YOUR DAY.

DATE: .... LOCATION: .... TODAY'S STAR RATING: ☆ ☆ ☆ ☆ ☆

TRAVELLED BY: ✈ □ PLANE   🚢 □ BOAT   🛣 □ ROAD   🪧 □ WALK   🎈 □ OTHER

WHERE DID I VISIT?

WHO WAS THERE?

WHAT I DISCOVERED?

WHO DID I MEET?

MY FAVOURITE THING WAS:

MY MOOD WAS   😄 □   🙂 □   😐 □   🙁 □   😎 □   😴 □

WEATHER   ☀ □   ⛅ □   🌦 □   ⛈ □   🌧 □   🌨 □

PICTURE OF THE DAY

DRAW, SKETCH OR STICK-IN A PICTURE OR KEEPSAKE OF YOUR DAY.

DATE:..................... LOCATION:.. TODAY'S STAR RATING: ☆☆☆☆☆

TRAVELLED BY: ✈ PLANE ☐ 🚢 BOAT ☐ 🛣 ROAD ☐ 🪧 WALK ☐ 🎈 OTHER ☐

WHERE DID I VISIT?

WHO WAS THERE?

WHAT I DISCOVERED?

WHO DID I MEET?

MY FAVOURITE THING WAS:

MY MOOD WAS 😄 ☐ 🙂 ☐ 😐 ☐ 🙁 ☐ 😎 ☐ 😴 ☐

WEATHER ☀ ☐ 🌤 ☐ 🌦 ☐ ⛈ ☐ 🌧 ☐ 🌨 ☐

PICTURE OF THE DAY

DRAW, SKETCH OR STICK-IN A PICTURE OR KEEPSAKE OF YOUR DAY.

DATE:...................... LOCATION:... TODAY'S STAR RATING: ☆ ☆ ☆ ☆ ☆

TRAVELLED BY: ✈ ☐ 🚢 ☐ 🛣 ☐ 🪧 ☐ 🎈 ☐
PLANE   BOAT   ROAD   WALK   OTHER

WHERE DID I VISIT?

WHO WAS THERE?

WHAT I DISCOVERED?

WHO DID I MEET?

MY FAVOURITE THING WAS:

MY MOOD WAS 😄 ☐ 🙂 ☐ 😐 ☐ 🙁 ☐ 😎 ☐ 😴 ☐

WEATHER ☀ ☐ ⛅ ☐ 🌥 ☐ ⛈ ☐ 🌧 ☐ 🌨 ☐

PICTURE OF THE DAY

DRAW, SKETCH OR STICK-IN A PICTURE OR KEEPSAKE OF YOUR DAY.

DATE:........................ LOCATION:.. TODAY'S STAR RATING: ☆☆☆☆☆

TRAVELLED BY: ✈ PLANE ☐ 🚢 BOAT ☐ 🛣 ROAD ☐ 🪧 WALK ☐ 🎈 OTHER ☐

WHERE DID I VISIT?

WHO WAS THERE?

WHAT I DISCOVERED?

WHO DID I MEET?

MY FAVOURITE THING WAS:

MY MOOD WAS 😄 ☐ 🙂 ☐ 😐 ☐ 🙁 ☐ 😎 ☐ 😴 ☐

WEATHER ☀ ☐ ⛅ ☐ 🌦 ☐ ⛈ ☐ 🌧 ☐ 🌨 ☐

PICTURE OF THE DAY

DRAW, SKETCH OR STICK-IN A PICTURE OR KEEPSAKE OF YOUR DAY.

DATE: .... LOCATION: .... TODAY'S STAR RATING: ☆☆☆☆☆

TRAVELLED BY: ✈ PLANE ☐ 🚢 BOAT ☐ 🛣 ROAD ☐ 🪧 WALK ☐ 🎈 OTHER ☐

WHERE DID I VISIT?

WHO WAS THERE?

WHAT I DISCOVERED?

WHO DID I MEET?

MY FAVOURITE THING WAS:

MY MOOD WAS 😄 ☐ 🙂 ☐ 😐 ☐ 🙁 ☐ 😎 ☐ 😴 ☐

WEATHER ☀ ☐ ⛅ ☐ 🌥 ☐ ⛈ ☐ 🌧 ☐ 🌨 ☐

PICTURE OF THE DAY

DRAW, SKETCH OR STICK-IN A PICTURE OR KEEPSAKE OF YOUR DAY.

DATE:............................ LOCATION:... TODAY'S STAR RATING: ☆ ☆ ☆ ☆ ☆

TRAVELLED BY: ✈ PLANE ☐ 🚢 BOAT ☐ 🛣 ROAD ☐ 🪧 WALK ☐ 🎈 OTHER ☐

WHERE DID I VISIT?

WHO WAS THERE?

WHAT I DISCOVERED?

WHO DID I MEET?

MY FAVOURITE THING WAS:

MY MOOD WAS 😄 ☐ 🙂 ☐ 😐 ☐ 🙁 ☐ 😎 ☐ 😴 ☐

WEATHER ☀ ☐ ⛅ ☐ 🌥 ☐ ⛈ ☐ 🌧 ☐ 🌨 ☐

PICTURE OF THE DAY

DRAW, SKETCH OR STICK-IN A PICTURE OR KEEPSAKE OF YOUR DAY.

DATE:.................. LOCATION:.. TODAY'S STAR RATING: ☆ ☆ ☆ ☆ ☆

TRAVELLED BY: ✈ ☐ 🚢 ☐ 🔥 ☐ 🪧 ☐ 🎈 ☐
PLANE   BOAT   ROAD   WALK   OTHER

WHERE DID I VISIT?

WHO WAS THERE?

WHAT I DISCOVERED?

WHO DID I MEET?

MY FAVOURITE THING WAS:

MY MOOD WAS 😄 ☐ 🙂 ☐ 😐 ☐ 🙁 ☐ 😎 ☐ 😴 ☐

WEATHER ☀ ☐ ⛅ ☐ 🌥 ☐ ⛈ ☐ 🌧 ☐ 🌨 ☐

PICTURE OF THE DAY

DRAW, SKETCH OR STICK-IN A PICTURE OR KEEPSAKE OF YOUR DAY.

DATE:........................ LOCATION:.. TODAY'S STAR RATING: ☆ ☆ ☆ ☆ ☆

TRAVELLED BY: ✈ ☐ 🚢 ☐ 🛣 ☐ 🪧 ☐ 🎈 ☐
PLANE   BOAT   ROAD   WALK   OTHER

WHERE DID I VISIT?

WHO WAS THERE?

WHAT I DISCOVERED?

WHO DID I MEET?

MY FAVOURITE THING WAS:

MY MOOD WAS 😄 ☐ 🙂 ☐ 😐 ☐ 🙁 ☐ 😎 ☐ 😴 ☐

WEATHER ☀ ☐ ⛅ ☐ 🌦 ☐ ⛈ ☐ 🌧 ☐ 🌨 ☐

PICTURE OF THE DAY

DRAW, SKETCH OR STICK-IN A PICTURE OR KEEPSAKE OF YOUR DAY.

DATE:........................ LOCATION:... TODAY'S STAR RATING: ☆☆☆☆☆

TRAVELLED BY: ✈ ☐ 🚢 ☐ 🛣 ☐ 🪧 ☐ 🎈 ☐
PLANE   BOAT   ROAD   WALK   OTHER

WHERE DID I VISIT?

WHO WAS THERE?

WHAT I DISCOVERED?

WHO DID I MEET?

MY FAVOURITE THING WAS:

MY MOOD WAS 😄 ☐ 🙂 ☐ 😐 ☐ 🙁 ☐ 😎 ☐ 😴 ☐

WEATHER ☀ ☐ ⛅ ☐ 🌦 ☐ ⛈ ☐ 🌧 ☐ 🌨 ☐

PICTURE OF THE DAY

DRAW, SKETCH OR STICK-IN A PICTURE OR KEEPSAKE OF YOUR DAY.

THE BEST TRIP